PROTECTION SPELLS

AN ENCHANTING SPELL BOOK TO CLEAR NEGATIVE ENERGY

Aurora Kane

WELLFLEET
PRESS

Introduction

How often do you feel protected?

In your home, in your workplace, while traveling, or in your spirit, you may experience a sense of unease creeping in like a dark cloud or a thick feeling of foreboding. Call it intuition, or your higher power, but protection spells, rituals, charms, and sigils can help not only enforce a feeling of safety, but help eliminate that dark energy from your person or your space.

Have you ever carried an item that was significant to you or symbolic and was meant to protect and watch over you? Maybe it's something special from a loved one that you wear, or a religious emblem, such as a cross or Star of David. If you have such an item or charm, that is a wonderful start; you are in the right mindset to embark on a journey of casting protection spells for yourself or loved ones. The spells in this book will not only cater to your level of confidence as a spellcaster, but build on it. Accessibility and comfort are key to any novice or expert witch. No matter where you are on your spellcasting path, the right spell for protection is here for you.

How Protection Spells are Used

Protection spells can be used for a variety of reasons, from peace of mind, feeling safe, bringing luck into your life, to countering a dark spell someone may have placed on you. A big part of casting for protection is making sure that you're centered. Being centered and focused will boost the efficacy of any spell. So, before you dive into this book, I want you to really ask yourself: *What do you need protection from? What do you need to heal from? What is your fondest wish? What kind of luck do you need?*

Sit with these questions; meditate on them. There's no set time limit to this. It can be minutes, hours, or even days, just make sure it's during a time period when it's quiet, you're centered, and you can focus. I encourage you to journal your answers. Journaling may feel like homework to some, but it is an integral part to spellwork. Journaling helps bring clarity to our intentions, and it makes it clear to the universe precisely what it is we're asking for. Think of journaling as a counterbalance to a spell, in a way. It will help strengthen your mind, and casting.

It's most important that you never stop learning and honing your skills.

The first chapter covers spells to protect your home. Your home is where you spend most of your time. It's where you can peel off the layers of your day and truly be yourself, where you care for your children, and where you host friends and family. So, it makes sense that you would want to fiercely protect this space from all negativity. You might want to protect your home from thieves, or maybe you want to preserve a positive force, or maybe yet, you want to chase negative energy out. Chapter one is here to guide you.

Chapter 2 deals with the prevention of harm. Too often we focus so much on what has happened, that we forget that many types of harm can simply be prevented. Call on Goddesses of Protection to rebalance energies in your home, create protective charms to carry with you to ensure a safe return, or use salt spells to create a protective barrier around your home. You don't have to banish negativity if you've already prevented it.

Chapter 3 tackles the important issue of preventing and healing illness. We've all fallen victim to the latest virus going around, or we've watched our loved ones suffer from ailments.

Most of us have also experienced emotional and spiritual illness through heartbreak, stress, or conflict. In this chapter, you will learn spells that can help soothe and prevent the scope of illness for both you and the ones you love. When illness is prevented, it makes room in your life for you to continue to grow, find gratitude for your blessings, and accomplish your dreams.

In the fourth and final chapter, you will find spells to bring you good luck. When your life is packed full of good fortune, there's simply no space for harm to creep in! Here you will use candle spells, charmed oils, and Goddess rituals to bring mystical luck to your life. Whether you're looking for luck at the casino, you're seeking good news, or you need to dispel a curse, chapter 4 has you covered.

By deciding to learn the spells in this book, you've also decided that you and your dwelling are worthy of protection. This book is here to help illuminate your divine path. May it bring you protection, promote healing and calm, and bring a little luck your way.

SO MOTE IT BE.*

1

Spells for the Home

THE ADVANTAGE OF SPELLS FOR home protection is that most of the ingredients can be found in or around your dwelling. From herbs in your spice cabinet, to nature's pantry of leaves, to pinecones and twigs, here you'll find spells to give you peace of mind that your home is surrounded by a mystical shield of protection.

There are many different kinds of protection. Maybe there's a positive energy you want to protect, like when you're hosting a party, and you want to "protect" the vibe from falling flat. Or maybe it's a more tangible kind of protection, like from property damage, theft, or harm. Depending on your situation, perhaps gossipy and/or busybody neighbors, friends, or coworkers plague you. Or maybe it boils down to wanting protection for the inhabitants of your space, to keep your belongs safe, your pets safe, and even your workspace safe, both physically and spiritually. No matter what kind of protection you're searching for, you'll be able to find a spell that suits your needs in this chapter.

With a focus on the home, the spells can be customized to apply to the places you inhabit, from trailers to hotel rooms to office spaces. Open your mind and use your creativity to explore these spells and make them not only work to protect, but to cater specifically to your needs.

While it is vital to protect your dwelling against all forms of harm, let's not forget about its inhabitants or those you want to depart from your space. Cast a spell of protection for your pets, chase away a pest invasion, banish evil spirits, invite the fairies in, cope with Mercury in Retrograde, and much more. When you need protection for your home, turn to these pages.

Salt Spell for Home Protection

Salt, especially Himalayan salt, is imbued with the Earth's energies. Combine salt with the Moon's divine energy for a powerful spell to protect your home.

Fill a small dish with salt and place it under the Full Moon's light overnight to blend the energies of the salt and the Moon. The next day, walking clockwise around your home's perimeter, or the perimeter of a room, carry the salt and say quietly or aloud:

Spell

Moon and Earth, join energy
to keep this home in sight,
That safe we be, no harm to see,
by daylight or by night.

Bid Evil Spirits Adieu

Doors and windows are prime entry spots for evil to lurk. Keep entryways and windows clean and clear by sprinkling a little Himalayan salt in each of their corners, and let sit for twenty-four hours to absorb negative energies. Imagine a white, cleansing light filtering the space as you sweep or vacuum any potential harm away. Once complete, take three deep breaths, exhaling from your mouth before saying quietly or aloud:

Spell

*This home is blessed by light of day
and charmed by dark of night.
Where love abounds
no evil is found
nor harmful agents fright.
With grains of salt and besom broom,
I cast you from this site.*

Pinecone Spell

Pinecones have long been associated with consciousness and enlightenment. The pineal gland, named after pinecones, affects our perception of light and has been called our "biological third eye." It connects to our intuition and our ability to both hear and be guided by our inner wisdom.

In nature, pinecones are strongholds of protection against bad weather and hungry animals, keeping seeds safe until it is time for them to grow. Pinecones can be placed in your space to lend their powerful protective capabilities to you while also serving as a reminder to turn to your own inner third eye.

Close your eyes and focus on wherever on your person you feel your third eye is located. Picture a light in the darkness radiating from that space within you and covering the entire outside of your dwelling. When you feel ready, say softly or aloud:

Spell

I trust the light I see within though darkness may abound.
I conjure this cocoon of light to keep us safe and sound.

Rosemary Fortification Ritual

While burning sage in the home is a well-known method of driving out negativity, this spell takes it a step further by sealing each room afterward with the fortifying qualities of rosemary.

After you've cleansed your space with a good smudging, take a cotton ball and lightly wet it with rosemary essential oil. Starting from the center of the home and working your way outward, dab the cotton ball of oil on each corner of every doorway in a clockwise motion. As you do this, chant:

Spell

Goddess-bless, Goddess-wise,
all who enter will respect me and mine or else leave in peace.

Keep Your Pet Safe

Our pets are part of our family, and we always want them to be safe and sound.

Set up a brown candle on your altar space. Place your pet's tag, collar, or toy in front of the candle. If your pet doesn't have those, you can use a bit of hair, feathers, scales, etc. that have naturally shed, along with a small piece of paper with your pet's name written in ink.

As you light the candle, envision your pet in a safe place surrounded by a cozy light. Conjure up all the wonderful, warm feelings you have for your pet, and say quietly or aloud:

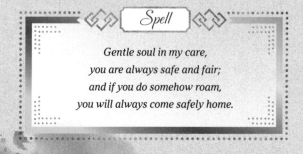

Spell

Gentle soul in my care,
you are always safe and fair;
and if you do somehow roam,
you will always come safely home.

New Year's Eve Entryway Spell

It is believed by the Irish that upon entering a new home, you must also leave through the same door to ensure luck flows into the home ... except at the witching hour on New Year's Eve, when in the front and out the back you must go to sweep in a lucky new year.

Set the tone for your home and year with a welcome mat or sign so that all who enter here feel love. Light a white candle and stare into its flame, centering your thoughts. Chant softly or aloud:

Spell

This home abounds with life and love and welcomes all who come.
For multiplied these joys do thrive when shared by more than one.
The love and laughter echo on and, yes, the house does smile.
Bless this house and all who come, be they woman, man, or child.

Obsidian Shield

Obsidian is known for cleansing spaces of negative energy by absorbing and neutralizing it. It acts as a barrier from people and situations that sap your positive energy and can be used to help sever ties with toxic relationships and circumstances.

Place an obsidian stone somewhere you can visualize a boundary. For a physical space, this can be by a doorway, windowpane, or other threshold. For an emotional boundary, place it within your reach in a place that holds comforting and safe sentiment for you.

Light a candle or incense with your preferred scent. Take a moment to be still and center yourself. As you let the smell fill the space around you, picture yourself untangling from negative energy as if it were an unraveling knot, then severing the cord.

When you feel ready, say quietly or aloud:

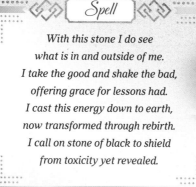

Spell

*With this stone I do see
what is in and outside of me.
I take the good and shake the bad,
offering grace for lessons had.
I cast this energy down to earth,
now transformed through rebirth.
I call on stone of black to shield
from toxicity yet revealed.*

Take a moment to write in your journal about the different sensations of where you are after completing this spell: smell, sight, touch, taste, and sound. Remember these sensations or revisit this journal entry when you need to feel grounded and safe from toxicity.

Keep Safe and Secure

Physical, emotional, and spiritual safety are basic rights in our homes. Let nothing threaten them—ever. Give the area in need of security a fresh smudging before chanting the following spell softly or aloud. If you feel you are in need of an extra layer of protection, perform this three times:

Spell

Let lock and key deter those who might intend me harm.
Let spirit guide who dwells inside protect this house with charm.
With earthly strength and heaven's might, I shroud myself in courage
That unseen dragons lying wait do slink away discouraged.

Banish Unwanted Pests

Be they mice under the stairs, birds eating your newly planted garden seeds, squirrels, deer, raccoons, skunks, or any other nuisances, pests are really just animals in the wrong places. No need to do them harm, but do lay down the law—and a hefty border of citrus peels, cayenne pepper, cinnamon, and other natural repellents. Place the repellants in a jar. Speak this incantation over the jar, gently rolling the jar between your hands as you do so. Then spread the repellants as a perimeter where needed.

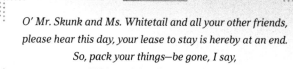

Spell

O' Mr. Skunk and Ms. Whitetail and all your other friends,
please hear this day, your lease to stay is hereby at an end.
So, pack your things—be gone, I say,
I bid you fair adieu, my friend.

Unfriending Spell

This is a spell to bring to light anyone who is harming you, whether it's deliberate or an unconscious action. Carry these charmed stones with you, and if someone's intention is harmful, they will fade from your life.

Gather a small black onyx to guard against negative energy, one small blue sodalite stone to distract negative people, and one red jasper to promote stability.

Rinse the stones in natural running water such as a creek, stream, or even a heavy rain. After they are cleansed, hold them in your hand and say quietly or aloud three times:

Spell

Oh Goddess Hecate, hear my plea,
Protect my head,
Protect my heart,
Protect my light.

Hidden Home Boundary

Regular, smooth river rocks conjure the grounding effect of the earth, and when they're in a line, the energy flows just like the water that shaped them. You can use any size or color of rocks, as long as they are smooth on one side.

Gather enough stones to circle your outdoor plants near doors or to line up on the ground underneath windows. With a paintbrush and clear-coat craft paint, paint a symbol of protection on the underside of each rock. It can be a pentacle, a rune, or any other symbol that resonates with you. Once all the stones are in place, stand in your home, close your eyes and mentally see a wave of protective energy rushing over the stones like a torrent of water. When you feel ready, say quietly or aloud:

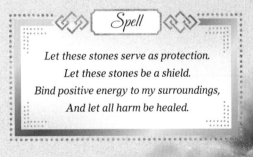

Spell

Let these stones serve as protection.
Let these stones be a shield.
Bind positive energy to my surroundings,
And let all harm be healed.

Genius Loci's Broom

The witch's broom is a powerful tool. While typically used to consecrate and cleanse spaces or to create energetic gateways during ritual work, it can also be used as a protection ward when kept stick-side down by the entrance of your home. "Genius Loci," stemming from Roman history, is the protective energy of and your connection to your sense of place. This spell uses what you have around you, your intuition, and your creativity to construct your own broom to keep your home safe and to ward away unwanted visitors.

The instructions for creating a Genius Loci Broom are simple:

1. Take a walk in your neighborhood, or your favorite woodsy place. Look at the things around you with the eyes of an artist looking for project materials. Fallen sticks and branches, dried grass, fallen palm fronds, or any natural materials that catch your eye. Collect what you feel Genius Loci is calling you to collect. Once home, place your materials on a cleansed sacred space.

2. Now, build your broom. The most common construction is one larger long stick with a bundle of smaller thinner sticks or dried plant matter tied around the bottom with a string, twine, or rope. Size, shape, and perfection don't matter; it's the symbolism that is most important. Add trinkets, crystals, talismans, or anything that will help raise the protective energy. During the building process, think about your home in its most ideal state: Free of negative energy, safe, powerful, contained, and harmonious.

Once completed, place the broom near your front door, stick-side down. You can also place it above your door horizontally.

Fast-Acting Protection Oil

This oil is a very powerful tool that will protect any item you anoint with it. Before beginning this spell, ask the deities to protect and keep safe anything this oil may touch. Charge your oil by setting it out in the light of a Waxing Moon for three nights. On the fourth day, it is ready to use.

Gather:

♦ Frankincense essential oil
♦ Rosemary essential oil
♦ Cinnamon essential oil or slivers of cinnamon bark
♦ Small dried bits of orange peel
♦ A carrier oil such as olive oil, almond oil, or coconut oil
♦ A 4 oz. bottle with cap or stopper

1. Slip the dried orange peel into the bottle.

2. Add four drops of frankincense oil.

3. Squeeze in three drops of rosemary oil.

4. Fill the bottle three-quarters full with your carrier oil, and put the cap on tightly.

Protective Bellarmine

The protective bellarmine, or "Witch's Jar," is one of the most common tools in witchcraft. Light a white candle anointed with protection oil. You will also need a black candle to seal the jar after it's closed.

Gather:

- 7 black peppercorns
- 7 whole cloves
- Cinnamon stick
- Peeled cloves of fresh garlic
- Odd number of bent pins to raise repellant energy
- 1 bay leaf with a word or sigil written on it. Burn and place the ashes in the jar.
- Generous pinch of crushed eggshells
- Generous pinch of salt

As you add each ingredient, envision them activating and generating strong protective and repellant energy. Once all the ingredients are added, fill the jar with vinegar nearly to the top, and put on the lid. Light your black candle and drip the wax on the top to seal it. Bury the sealed jar in your desired location.

Preserve This Home

In the same way you can use your kitchen to preserve the culinary magic of fresh herbs, you can also use the magical properties of herbs to help preserve your home. Keep your home safe from negative energies, illness, strife, and bad luck. Blend your fresh, finely-chopped herbs of choice with a bit of olive oil to form a paste. Freeze the paste in ice cube trays. Once solid, transfer to an airtight freezer bag and keep frozen for up to six months. Each time you toss one into sauces, soups, and stews give a simple nod to their benefits by saying quietly or aloud:

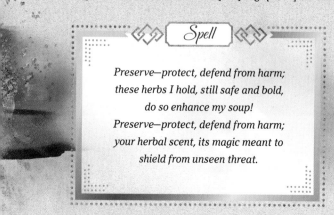

Spell

Preserve—protect, defend from harm;
these herbs I hold, still safe and bold,
do so enhance my soup!
Preserve—protect, defend from harm;
your herbal scent, its magic meant to
shield from unseen threat.

Lokahi Harmonious Home

In Indigenous Hawaiian healing practices, the word "lokahi" represents harmony with the world and people around you. The "Lokahi Triangle" speaks to physical, mental, and spiritual balance. To honor the sacred number 3, and to invite that balance, all ingredients included in this spell should be added in 3s. 3 pinches, 3 drops.

In a sachet pouch, intentionally add:

♦ Chamomile for serenity and calm
♦ Garden sage for purification
♦ Bay leaf with your intention written on it
♦ 3 drops lavender essential oil
♦ 3 drops peppermint essential oil

Once completed, tie the sachet closed and place it hidden in any part of your home that has been feeling unharmonious or tense.

Angel Protection Charm

In numerology, angel numbers are repeating sequences of numbers that you might see randomly throughout your day. It is said that this is a sign from your angel that they are present, you are protected, and your desires have been heard. In this spell, we will be honoring the angel number 4 and its message that your angel is working hard to offer you love, support, guidance, and protection.

Gather:

♦ 1 piece of amethyst for protection, healing, and purification

♦ 1 item that represents protection to you. It could be a picture, a word written on a piece of paper, or a charm or bead shaped like a skull or a weapon. Let your intuition guide you.

♦ 1 generous pinch of crushed eggshells for strong protection

♦ 1 bay leaf to actualize your intent and to ward off negative forces. Write your intent distilled to 1–3 words on the leaf. It could just say "Protection" or "Protection from [X]". You can also use a sigil instead of words.

Add each ingredient into the sachet. As you handle each item, imagine it surrounded by a warm glow to fill it with the intention that they will all come together to create a protective shield that will allow you to move throughout your day without negative influences or affectation.

As you carry your protective charm with you, keep an eye out for the number 4, especially if it's in a sequence. This is your signal that the charm is working and that your angel is watching with a fiercely protective eye.

Repel Evil Spirits

After an argument, an illness, losing a job, or other adversity in your home, it's likely you'll feel the stagnant energy affecting everything you do.

Select the herbs you'd like to work with and place them on your altar as an offering to Saturn. Close your eyes and visualize first your altar, then the room, then the whole house filled with clean bright light. When ready, say quietly or aloud:

Spell

With these herbs plucked from the Earth
and filled with the power to banish,
I cast these words with most fervent urge
to cleanse, clear, and halt evil spirits.
With power of their leaves, I restore peace and ease
that home does repair, heal, and flourish.

Breathe Easy

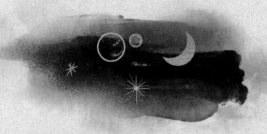

Boston ferns are known to detoxify the air. Keep one in your home anywhere a little fresh air—and sense of security—will help you breathe easier. Include ferns in any bouquets to amplify the message intended. Use in spells calling for protection from unseen evil. Grow for their soothing visual qualities. Use a frond to sprinkle Moon water on your altar to boost protective spells.

Anytime you feel the need to use fern, say quietly or aloud:

Spell

O' fairest fern, I call on you to spread your fairy wings to keep me safe from evil spells and other harmful things.

Runic Banishing Spell

This spell utilizes the power of Algiz, an Elder Futhark rune, to assist in banishing negative energy and influences.

Algiz Rune

Defense; Ward off Evil;
Shield/Guardian;
Connection with gods;
Awakening; Higher Life

Gather:

♦ A black candle
♦ Sharp carving tool
♦ Your own potion of protection oil
♦ Patchouli essential oil
♦ Lavender essential oil
♦ Salt

1. After a few deep breaths to align your energy, use your sharp tool to carve the rune Algiz on the surface of your candle while chanting the name to activate its energy. Continue until your candle is completely covered with the symbol.

2. Anoint the candle with your protective oil.

3. In a cleansed receptacle, mix 8 drops each:

   ♦ Patchouli for protection, courage, spiritual growth
   ♦ Lavender for purification

4. Anoint your candle with the mixture.

5. Light the candle in a firesafe vessel and surround with a protective circle of salt.

6. Charge your candle by speaking your intent; use your intuition and speak from your heart.

Let it burn out completely, or blow it out to end the spell.

Soothe Mental Anguish

Look to the Full Moon to offer her most protective charms when searching for ways to keep your home safe from lingering mental anguish, especially after an argument. To conjure good mental health, cast this spell while walking from room to room throughout the home where people gather while chanting quietly or aloud:

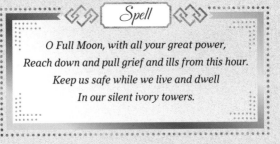

Spell

O Full Moon, with all your great power,
Reach down and pull grief and ills from this hour.
Keep us safe while we live and dwell
In our silent ivory towers.

Keep Safe On the Road

Both hematite and tiger's eye naturally carry the magical attributes of protection and grounding. Hematite is especially good for sharpening your senses and clearing your mind, while tiger's eye keeps your focus steady and strong. If you experience "road rage," dissolve it by utilizing blue lace agate.

♦ In a black sachet, the color of banishing, protection, grounding, and safety, place one of each of these three stones.
♦ For 5 minutes before you embark on your commute, close your eyes and visualize a glowing white protective dome of light surrounding your vehicle.
♦ After you've done this for three mornings, place the bundle in your glove box, your knapsack, or pocket.

You are now tuned into the effects of these three stones and have sealed a safe arrival.

Protection from
Bad Influences

Whether you have a loved one that continues to make dangerous life choices, or you think evil may be working against them, this spell is a powerful shield comprised of your loving thoughts.

With a blue pen, write the full name of your person in the center of a piece of paper. Keep the pen down on the paper at the end of the name and continue writing all the good qualities they have. The writing should curve under their name, and all their positive actions and traits should form a spiral moving outward, clockwise on the paper. Don't lift the pen from the paper until you've run out of things to write.

Now, set aside the blue pen and pick up a gold one. From the end of their name, trace a golden path around the words, around the spiral until you reach the edge of the paper.

Fold the paper and put it in a safe place, occasionally recharging it with loving energy by holding the paper and speaking the name of the person, and then the qualities you've written.

Garden Fairy Protection

A traditional witch's garden plant, foxglove is purely ornamental, as its toxic nature can harm if ingested. The origin of its name stems from the fact that the flowers resemble the fingers of a glove and refers to the "good folk," or rather, the fairies who dwell deep within the forest.

Here, you will plant foxglove in your garden to draw the interest of fairies and offer them a natural dwelling. At your local plant nursery, obtain one or all purple, yellow, and white foxglove plants. Prepare the dirt in your garden by running your palms over it lightly while focusing your intent on protection. Invite the fairies and ask for their protection by saying quietly or aloud:

Spell

Where unseen evil bides its time to unleash all its woe,
I call on foxglove's warning bells, a powerful farrow.
Swift fairies swarm to guard this home, an answer to this call,
Please keep us safe from evil eye, dark spirits, and fleshly maul.

Bless This Home Ritual

The New Moon, a phase of new beginnings, is an ideal time
to bless and cleanse your space. This two-step ritual first clears
negative energy, then fills the space with positive,
joyful intentions.

To cleanse the space, burn a sage wand fortified with eucalyptus,
paying special attention to corners, closets, and doorways.

On your altar, gather salt, bread, wine, and a few coins.

Breathe naturally and imagine the air, dark and foggy,
beginning to become crystal clear. When you feel ready, say
quietly or aloud:

Spell

With salt for protection, bread for health, wine for happy times,
I cast these coins about my realm—life's riches will be mine.
Please bless this house for in its midst, life lived will be sublime.

Safe & Sound Oil

Black pepper has been used by witches for centuries to banish negativity and protect from evil spirits.

Gather:

- ◆ 3 slightly crushed, whole black peppercorns
- ◆ 10 drops of each essential oil:

- • Geranium
- • Lemon
- • Frankincense
- • Neroli
- • Sandalwood

Fill your glass receptacle with your carrier oil, leaving about 1–2 inches of space at the top. Add each ingredient while visualizing negativity bouncing off of your spiritual umbrella and say:

Spell

O sacred pepper, I call on you to keep me safe and sound.
Banish evil spirits and bring blessings that abound.
Soteria, infuse this potion with all your godly charm,
So all who use it to anoint will surely evade harm.

Clean Heart, Clean Hands

Here, you will make a protective hand soap for every day use.

♦ Drop a healthy pinch of dried basil, mint, and thyme into a small, clear jar.

♦ Fill the jar with water, close the lid, and set in the sun to steep and soak in her powerful energy.

♦ Once the water has reached the color and delicious scent of a rich herbal tea, pour out ¼ cup of liquid directly into a liquid soap dispenser.

♦ Fill the dispenser the rest of the way with an unscented or lightly scented liquid soap, attach the cap, and shake.

Any time you wash your hands, chant:

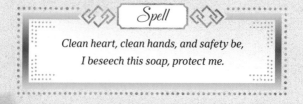

Spell

Clean heart, clean hands, and safety be,
I beseech this soap, protect me.

Freeze Out Gossip

While this spell blocks gossip, it also conjures Eirene, the personification of peace, to permeate your spirit and home. In a cleansed, freezer-safe vessel, intentionally add:

♦ A small piece of paper with the gossiper's name written on it; a picture of them will also suffice.
♦ 1 piece of orange peel
♦ 1 whole clove
♦ 1 black peppercorn
♦ 1 pinch of ground cinnamon

Slowly fill the vessel with water. Once full, seal and place in the back of your freezer. When it is fully frozen, the spell has blocked gossip. Chant:

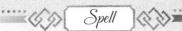

Spell

Listen one, listen all, to my commanding incantation.
Seal your lips, freeze your tongue from speaking your damnation.
I release you now, I cut the cord, I wrap your words in chains,
I conjure Eirene and all her charm to restore my peace again.

Uncrossing Spell

An uncrossing spell is used for the removal of a curse (or cross that has been laid upon you) that causes roadblocks of negative energy in your life.

The number 13 brings luck and success, the opposite of a curse. Here we'll use 13 ingredients to conjure these positive forces.

In a cleansed jar, gather:

- Sage
- Mugwort
- Witch's black salt
- Clove
- Thyme
- Chamomile
- Eucalyptus
- Mint
- Patchouli
- Rose petals
- Rosemary
- Basil
- Lemongrass

Fill the herbed jar the rest of the way with carrier oil. Allow it to sit in a dark place for at least 3 weeks, shaking the jar every 5 days or so. This oil should only be used to anoint candles, tools, and talismans, and should not be worn or diffused.

Mercury in Retrograde Potion

When Mercury, the planet of clarity and communication, goes into retrograde, *everything* seems to go wrong. This oil-potion will help protect you from the negative influences of Mercury in retrograde and can be used to anoint candles, diffuse into the air, or wear dabbed on your throat and sacral chakras.

In a cleansed jar add frankincense, sweet orange, and ylang-ylang essential oils. Sprinkle in dried sage and orange peels.

Sit quietly in a dark, comfortable space and conjure images of clear and concise communication, no confusion, and the ability to move with dignity and grace.

Spell

O Mercury, god of clarity, messenger to the gods,
I call on thee, retrograde free, to help me beat these odds.
Through my door, with spirits high, I banish all confusion,
And shield my soul, my spirit whole, from negative intrusion.

Protection from Negative Thinking

In this modern world, so often we find that we constantly compare ourselves to what we see in advertising, television, and social media. We may feel insufficient and judge ourselves too harshly, blocking our intuition and magical abilities. This oil can be used in any spellwork to bind self-doubt or limiting beliefs that you can't seem to shake from your thoughts.

Gather:

- Ground cinnamon
- Dried mint
- Dried rosemary
- Whole black peppercorns
- Dried chili flakes or ground cayenne pepper
- Fresh lemon rind
- Freshly peeled cloves of garlic

In a cleansed stove-top pot, add enough of your preferred carrier oil to fill your chosen glass vessel, and at least 5 tbsp. of ground cinnamon. On low heat, allow to warm, stirring occasionally in a counterclockwise fashion. Once heated through, remove from heat to allow to cool slightly for 5–10 minutes.

While it cools, add the ingredients to your jar. Use your intuition to decide how much or how little of each ingredient to add. Once cool enough that you can comfortably hold the jar, pour your warmed carrier oil infused with cinnamon over the other ingredients and fill nearly to the top. Do not put the lid on until the mixture is completely cool. Hold the jar to your solar plexus and say quietly or aloud:

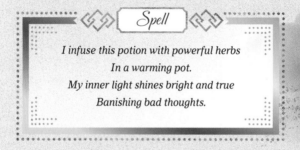

Spell

I infuse this potion with powerful herbs
In a warming pot.
My inner light shines bright and true
Banishing bad thoughts.

Once completed, store in a dark, cool place for 1 week and strain before using it in your magic practice. If you feel self-doubt creeping in while preparing a spell or just in your daily life, anoint your altar, your tools, and dab on the inside of your wrists. Keep negative thoughts at bay by dabbing on the top crest of windows, doorways, the head of your bed, and even your heart chakra.

Hoodoo Florida Water Tincture

Florida Water is a mystical alcohol-based perfume water originally created in the early 1800s. It was later adopted by Hoodoo, New Orleans Voodoo, and Santeria practices and has persisted as a staple cleansing tool in modern witchcraft. It can be used to anoint magical tools or as a floor wash to cleanse your altar space and home. You can also splash it on your hands to wash away negative energies and to prepare yourself for ritual work.

Gather:

- 2 cinnamon sticks
- 13 cloves
- 4 sprigs fresh rosemary
- 1 ½ handfuls fresh mint
- 1 handful fresh basil
- ⅓ cup dried jasmine flowers
- ½ cup dried lavender buds
- Rind of 1 navel orange
- Petals and hips of 10 bloomed roses
- Vodka
- Rose essential oil
- Jasmine essential oil
- Bergamot essential oil

Aside from the essential oils, add each ingredient to a stove-top cauldron. As you do, visualize their unique powers as a tinted light glowing around each of them: purple light for lavender, forest green for rosemary, bright green for basil, and so forth. Cover your ingredients with the vodka until the cauldron is full.

1. On medium-low heat, bring your mixture to a soft, bubbling boil to heat through. Reduce to low heat and let simmer for about 30 minutes, stirring counterclockwise frequently to raise releasing energy. After 30 minutes, remove from heat and let cool, then strain out the plant material.

2. To the strained, slightly warm liquid, add 21 drops each of the rose, jasmine, and bergamot essential oils.

3. Close the lid and shake vigorously, visualizing how well this water will cleanse out unwanted energies and will move them sweetly, but forcefully, out of your space.

Leave to cool on your altar or in full moonlight. This potion can keep for up to one year at room temperature.

Ancestral Protection Oil

This enchanted oil summons the watchful protectiveness of your ancestors. With modern witchcraft, we often forget that the energy of our ancestors is still with us and radiates all around us. Ancestral wisdom, familial care, foresight, and cosmic assistance can be conjured with this potion, especially when added to your other spells. This potion is most effective when made during the Waxing Moon.

Before you get started, create your own sigil on either paper or a bay leaf, on which you will scribe something personalized but similar to, "My ancestors protect me" in order to bind your intention.

Gather:

- 3 cloves
- Frankincense resin
- 1 clear quartz crystal
- 4 drops bergamot essential oil
- 4 drops ylang-ylang essential oil
- 3 drops lavender essential oil
- A white candle

Fill a cleansed glass jar with carrier oil then add your items, including your sigil, one by one. Fasten the lid and briefly shake. Hold the filled jar to your heart chakra while visualizing your ancestors gathered around you in a protective circle, holding hands.

Allow the vision of the comforting, protective energy and divine guidance of your ancestors to swirl up through you and into the bottle.

Mindfully carve your sigil into the white candle until it is fully covered. Anoint the candle with the sacred potion of your ancestors, and place in a firesafe vessel on your altar. Once lit, say quietly or aloud:

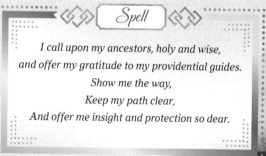

Spell

I call upon my ancestors, holy and wise,
and offer my gratitude to my providential guides.
Show me the way,
Keep my path clear,
And offer me insight and protection so dear.

2

Spells to
Prevent
Harm

IN THIS CHAPTER, YOU WILL LEARN and practice spells that will help prevent the negative energies that cause harm and replace them with protective energies. May this chapter help promote peace and serenity in your life and bring calm to your well-being as harm and negative energies are warded away from you.

Not all harm is insidious in nature; it could be something as seemingly inconsequential as jet lag or a bad ankle sprain. *Harm* refers to things that cause a spike downward or a splinter in your mental or physical wellbeing.

Any type of harm can be a horrible distraction. Think of harm in the broader sense of the word. What has been harmful in your day to day? This can include things like procrastination or a toxic relationship.

Here you will find spells that will help prevent or assuage harm no matter where you are. You'll find spells for your home, protective jars to carry with you, and spells for safe travel, to name a few.

This chapter will also teach you how to make charmed items that can be used in any spell practice and add a boost of power to your spells. Sprinkle Witch's Black Salt over your home protection candle to enhance its powers, create a protective wreath to hang in your home, repel negativity with mirror boxes, and conjure a protective cloak around your children or pets, to name a few. Whatever your goals for protection from harm may be, these spells will not only promote protection, but enhance it.

So mote it be.

Many Safe Returns

Make a simple travel spell bag to tuck into your luggage, purse, pocket, or glove compartment to ensure a safe return home.

For Protection	For Calm	For Jet Lag
Acorn	Chamomile	Gentian
Angelica	Frankincense	Ginseng
Basil	Lavender	Mugwort
Comfrey	Lemon balm	Passionflower

Fold them into a bundle, and tie it tightly with a white ribbon, the color of spiritual purity. Feel gratitude for the protection afforded by the herbs. Say quietly or aloud:

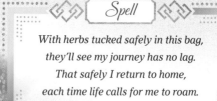

Spell

With herbs tucked safely in this bag,
they'll see my journey has no lag.
That safely I return to home,
each time life calls for me to roam.

Repel Danger Emergency Spell

Do you feel that someone might be preparing to do you harm? If you feel in danger, either spiritually or physically, or someone is bringing negative energy into your life, don't wait! This fast-acting spell can be uttered at any time, no matter your physical circumstance. It can be said under your breath at the grocery store, school, work, or anywhere else you feel danger lurking. Restore order and balance to your world with the Moon's cleansing energies. With a clear threat in mind, and intentions focused, say quietly or aloud:

Spell

Goddess Moon, warrior of night, I plead my case to thee.
With threat of harm, extend your arms, safely encircled I be.
Protect and soothe, give strength to fight what does not strengthen me.

Pause a moment to acknowledge the Moon for her strength and feel the determination in you grow. Us witches work in tandem with the physical world, so if you feel a serious threat, also call the authorities.

Goddess Ma'at Prayer

When we know what's right but feel unprepared for the fight, a goddess whose influence includes strength, truth, and power can be our best ally. In times like these, we call on Goddess Ma'at to help bring the clarity and courage we need to do the right thing. Don't be afraid to ask Ma'at for help.

Spell

In times of darkness, bring your light.
In times of fear, clear my sight.
Goddess Ma'at, stand with me
to give me courage to fight the fight.
For peace I pray and strength to stand
for what is right, which will demand
a courage so deep I fear I'll fail,
but with your help I will prevail.

On your altar, light a white candle and lay gold and silver items around it as an offering of gratitude to the amenable Goddess.

Protective Wreath

The wreath, an unending circle, symbolizes eternity and the cycle of the seasons.

Use these protective herbs to protect your home with the energies of the seasons:

Angelica *(Spring, Summer)*
Basil *(Summer)*
Bay laurel *(Spring)*
Chives *(Spring, Fall)*
Dill *(Spring, Fall)*

Holly *(Winter)*
Rosemary *(Fall, Winter)*
Sage *(Fall, Winter)*
Star anise *(Winter)*
Witch hazel *(Fall, Winter)*

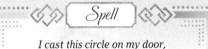

Spell

I cast this circle on my door,
with herbs so rich and deep in lore,
that from all ills protected be,
my home will ne'er be harmed nor poor.

The Many Lives of Bay Laurel

Bay leaves offer strength, protection, and purification. They are also used to aid healing and to fuel good wishes, glory, and change.

Hang bay branches near the entryways to your home to purify the air. Dip bay sprigs in Moon water to sprinkle over your altar for cleansing. Write wishes on bay leaves and safely burn them to send your intentions into the Universe. Add whole leaves to soups and stews to boost not only depth of flavor but also intuition and strength. Tuck into sachets or decorate a wreath to honor your glory. Tuck a sprig of bay under your pillow to encourage deep rest.

Spell

With bay in hand, I proudly stand before the goddess realm
to thank you for the path you've strewn with guidance, grit, and more
for glory to the sisterhood of those who came before.

Breaking Bad Habits

Chives season life with joy and courage as well as guard against illness and harmful spirits. They're effective at helping break bad habits, especially ones that cause lasting physical harm.

Begin by making yourself a salad of all your favorite healthy ingredients. Focus on freshness and bright colors. Lightly dress, or simply sprinkle with lemon juice and add some torn herbs.

Lay your salad on your altar alongside a bundle of long chive sprigs. As many times as your intuition commands, pick up a single sprig, tie it in a knot, then break it in half while chanting:

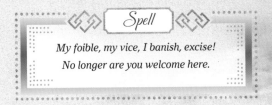

Spell

My foible, my vice, I banish, excise!
No longer are you welcome here.

Sprinkle chopped fresh chives over the top of the salad. Eat the salad mindfully, really feeling the healthy nutrients replacing all negative habits.

Pantheon of Protection

During challenging times, you may need strength, you might need wisdom, and you might also need justice. Whatever powers your situation calls for, now is the time to call on an assemblage of gods and goddesses, known as a pantheon. These allies will combine their protective energies and unique powers to keep you safe while navigating the path forward.

On your altar, light a dark blue candle, the color of the gods. Warm your hands by the flame and imagine this is the cloak that has been wrapped around you. When ready, say quietly or aloud:

Spell

I call on the pantheon of deities,
Rise up, join hands, raise energies.
For evil lurks and roams this world,
misdeeds have been so long endured.
I plead with you whom I invoke,
To wrap me in your golden cloak.

Goddess Selene
Rebalancing Ritual

Selenite's name honors the Greek Goddess of the Moon, Selene. Its cleansing energies, when paired with the energies of the New and Full Moons, are particularly effective to wipe the slate clean and clearly see the path forward. To activate the protective powers of the Goddess Selene, place your selenite crystal in a shallow hole in the earth, under the light of the Full or New Moon. Gently cover it with loose earth while saying softly or aloud:

Spell

When doubt and fear do lurk too near, sweep shadows out the door.

No harm shall come to anyone and peace shall be restored.

Be bright of day, or darkness loom, all enemies do cower.

With Moon above and crystal charm, I am strong and am in power.

In the morning, unearth the selenite stone. Carry it with you to evoke its protective power everywhere you go.

Sacred Circle

Sometimes it can be difficult to tell if our tumultuous emotions are really ours, or if we're absorbing the negative energies of those around us. This ritual will help define where the boundary between the self and the other lies.

Gather a ball of yarn, a candle, and a single match.

1. In the cleared space, unravel the yarn around you to make a circle.

2. Light the candle. With your eyes open, take a few deep breaths and notice the floor beneath you. Explore only the space within the circle, letting the candle's glow cast a natural emphasis on the boundary between your space and the space beyond you. Say aloud:

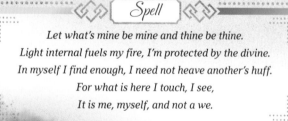

Spell

Let what's mine be mine and thine be thine.
Light internal fuels my fire, I'm protected by the divine.
In myself I find enough, I need not heave another's huff.
For what is here I touch, I see,
It is me, myself, and not a we.

Energy Shield

If you need to be around people who sap you of your energy or leave you feeling deflated afterwards, performing this ritual ahead of time can offer you extra protection in maintaining your own energy.

1. Begin by gathering together chocolate to invoke the power of your guides, a small glass of pure water, and a candle.

2. Place the chocolate and water on your altar as an offering and light the candle to call in your guides.

3. Set your intention of feeling safe and protected. Close your eyes and bring your awareness first inward, then slowly expand your awareness outward into a growing light swelling around you.

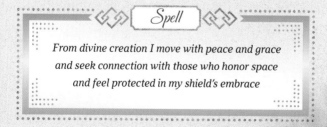

Spell

From divine creation I move with peace and grace
and seek connection with those who honor space
and feel protected in my shield's embrace

Veritas Honesty Spell

Here we call on Veritas, the Goddess of Truth.

1. On your altar, place a sheet of paper, a lit blue candle to represent truth, a black marker, 3 small black stones, and a freezer-safe receptacle.

2. On the piece of paper, write the name of the liar three times with the black marker.

3. Fold the paper lengthways away from you, then twist it three times.

4. Place the twisted paper in the freezer-safe container, along with the three small black stones. Pour water over them until covered.

As you seal the container and place it in the freezer, say softly:

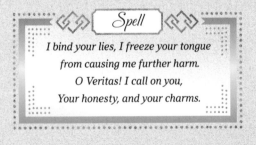

Spell

I bind your lies, I freeze your tongue
from causing me further harm.
O Veritas! I call on you,
Your honesty, and your charms.

Bedtime Anxiety Ritual

This pre-bedtime ritual can help to calm your racing mind.
Gather:

- Four pocket-sized mirrors
- Cedar oil
- Rosemary oil
- ½ cup almond oil

1. Lay the 4 mirrors out on your altar.

2. In a bottle, pour in the almond oil and mix in two drops
   each of the essential oils.

3. Dip your finger in the oil and draw a pentacle on each
   mirror's surface, while chanting:

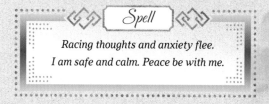

Spell

Racing thoughts and anxiety flee.
I am safe and calm. Peace be with me.

Place the mirrors in each corner of the bedroom, facing the
wall so all negativity is reflected back before it can enter your
dwelling as you sleep.

Toxic Work Environment Spell

When someone is creating a toxic work environment, use this spell to block the torment. Cloves are a powerful ally in repelling evil and preventing harm. Oranges have an energetic magical profile that summons love, improves luck, and manifests prosperity.

1. Make a small sachet filled with cloves and dried orange peel pieces, and conceal it at your workstation, preferably in a desk drawer or by your office door. If you work from home, keep it by your laptop or tablet.

2. Each time you sit down for the day to work, thank Lakshmi, the Hindu Goddess of luck, prosperity and, wealth for your bountiful career.

3. When you need a boost, smell the sachet and visualize a tangle of cloves and oranges surrounding your workspace, protecting you from harm and blessing you with productivity and success.

Any negative intentions sent to you from coworkers or other professionals will be stuck in that tangle and dissolve.

Foiled Enemy Spell

If you find yourself in constant conflict with an enemy, use this spell to defuse and confuse them so no harm comes to you.

Gather:

♦ Powdered or dried valerian root
♦ A photo print of your enemy who wishes you harm
♦ A length of aluminum foil, just large enough to cover your hand

Lay out the foil on your altar with the shiny side facing up.
On the photo, draw a large evil eye on their forehead. Place it on the top half of the foil. Sprinkle the valerian root on the photo while chanting:

Spell

Get away, stay away.
Your hatred has failed.
Chase your own tail.

Fold the foil upward as this spell moves harm away from you, and fold down every side until the foil forms a sealed packet.

Morning Light

Each morning, as you get ready for your day, stand in the sunlight with your feet apart and arms outstretched.

Take a deep, mindful breath and exhale.

Close your eyes and visualize a wave of blue energy washing up and around you, from your feet to your head.

Take a deep, mindful breath and exhale.

Imagine white protective energy swirling around you from all sides, forming a soft bubble around your body.

Take a deep, mindful breath and exhale.

Envision pure, golden energy from angelic sources pouring down on you, forming a glowing exterior of power and protection.

Take one last deep, mindful breath and slowly exhale.

Protection from Illness

Garlic protects from more than just vampires! It can add longevity to your life by boosting your immune system, detoxing your body, and lowering bad cholesterol. It also is a grounding vegetable, grown deep in the earth, that can strengthen your relationship to deep nourishment.

To protect your household from illness, hang garlic around your house, taking extra care to place it by doorways, windows, and spaces where people come together in conversation. As you hang your bundles of garlic, say quietly or aloud:

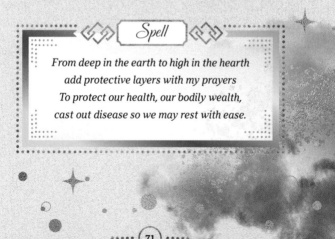

Spell

From deep in the earth to high in the hearth
add protective layers with my prayers
To protect our health, our bodily wealth,
cast out disease so we may rest with ease.

Witch's Black Salt

A blessed salt is highly protective and absorbs negative influences when included in your spellwork or when sprinkled around the perimeters of your home. The main ingredients in Witch's Black Salt are salt, activated charcoal, and incense ash.

Gather your ingredients and grind them in your mortar and pestle until fully combined. If you find yourself inspired, feel free to customize your blend by adding protective herbs or oils.

In any area of your home, your office, or any other dwelling, create a trap to absorb negative energy by sprinkling a small pinch of your witch's salt as you enter, or place in a small bowl in an unassuming place. Switch it out once a week by dumping the old salt in the toilet and flushing, imagining all of the negative energy that was absorbed into that salt being whisked far away from you.

Persephone's Incense

Peresephone suffers no fools, and neither should you.

In your mortar and pestle, grind dried lavender, rose petals, white willow bark, mint, and myrrh.

When thoroughly mixed, add the following essential oils:

- Grapefruit
- Peppermint
- Rose
- Frankincense
- Lavender
- Sandalwood

To activate the energy, hold your hands over the mixture and say:

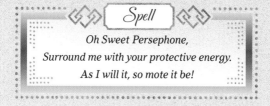

Spell

Oh Sweet Persephone,
Surround me with your protective energy.
As I will it, so mote it be!

Place a charcoal disc in a heat-safe vessel, light it, and wait for the disc to turn completely white. Then, add pinches of your loose incense to the very center of the disk.

Karmic Mirror Box

The intent of this spell is to encourage karma to balance whatever negative energy a particular person is outputting.

You can use any type of box in any size. If you have mirrors, place one on all sides on the inside of your box, including the inside of the lid.

Write the name of the person you wish to target on a piece of paper, fold it away from you 3 times while turning counterclockwise, and say quietly or aloud:

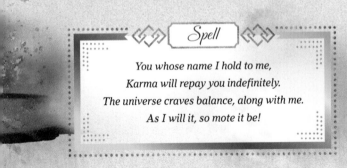

Spell

You whose name I hold to me,
Karma will repay you indefinitely.
The universe craves balance, along with me.
As I will it, so mote it be!

Place the paper in the box and close the lid. Put the box somewhere secret.

Divine Path Protection Jar

This jar is a shield around your manifestations and protects from influences that would deviate you from your divine path.

To begin, write on a piece of paper your intention to protect your workings, your manifestations, and your self-actualization, then place it at the bottom of your jar.

On top of paper, add:

- Eggshells
- Witch's black salt
- Ground ginger
- Whole peppercorns
- Whole cloves
- Star anise
- Bay leaves
- Cinnamon stick
- White vinegar
- Black candle

Fill the jar of ingredients almost to the top with white vinegar, draw a pentacle on the inside of the lid for extra protection, and close it tight. Light a black candle and drop wax over to seal your intent inside.

Pentacle Protection Wash

Rosemary is one of many great multiuse herbs that every witch should have on hand. Along with bringing prosperity and helping to strengthen memory, it's also a powerful addition to any protection spell.

To make this simple wash:

1. Pour boiling water into a mug and add at least 3 generous spoonfuls of dried rosemary,

2. Allow to steep until completely cool and strain out the herbs.

3. Starting with the farthest door or window, dip the index finger of your right hand in the wash and draw a protective pentacle on it.

4. Work your way towards the front of your house doing the same thing on all windows, both in and outside.

Hecate Protection Incense

Hecate, the Queen of Witches, is the protector of the home. This spell calls in the powerful energy Hecate offers to protect and guide you. In your mortar and pestle, grind bay leaves, rose petals, lavendar, and mugwort.

Once fully mixed, add essential oils:

- ♦ Rose
- ♦ Frankincense
- ♦ Lavender

Hold your hands over the mixture and say quietly or aloud:

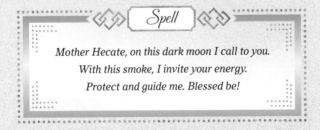

Spell

Mother Hecate, on this dark moon I call to you.
With this smoke, I invite your energy.
Protect and guide me. Blessed be!

Light a charcoal disk in a heat-safe vessel, wait for it to turn entirely white, and then add the loose incense to the center of the disk to burn.

Witch's Knot Intuition Spell

The purpose of this spell is to remove and trap any negative influences or limiting beliefs and banish them to clear space to strengthen your intuition.

Gather one long piece of cord, string, twine, or rope. Using your intuition, say a quiet blessing over the cord. Starting from about one or two inches from one end, form a simple knot, but don't tie it tight immediately. Hold the loose knot close to your mouth, with one hand on either side of the knot, and as you pull the knot tight, whisper whatever limiting belief or negative influence that is affecting you into the knot.

Once finished, you can throw the cord away, or cover it with moon water and place in the back of your freezer.

Vulnerability
Protection Bath

There are times when we feel especially vulnerable and sensitive, but can't really explain why. Maybe you're reacting to a moon cycle, maybe you've been under some undo stress, or maybe you feel vulnerable because of something spiritual going on that you're not aware of. You can bathe in this essential oil mixture as often as desired to strengthen your psychic awareness and to protect you from any type of potential attacks—spiritual, emotional, physical, or psychological.

Into a bathtub filled with warm water, add the following essential oils:

♦ Rosemary ♦ Frankincense
♦ Lavender ♦ Geranium

Swirl the water with your right hand counterclockwise 3 times, activating the intent that this bath will strengthen and protect you. Step in and soak for as long as you want.

All Purpose Protection Powder

This magical powder uses resins and powdered ingredients to create a strong protective shield that can be put in a sachet and carried on you as a protection charm, sprinkled around the perimeter of your home, or used to create a protective circle around you for ritual work.

In a mortar and pestle, finely grind:

- Sea salt
- Dragon's blood resin
- Frankincense resin
- Sandalwood powder
- Ground cumin
- Ground ginger
- Ground cinnamon

Once fully ground and combined, keep in an air-tight jar. You may need to stir it on occasion, as resins can start to gum up again over time.

Wash Away Distractions

Whenever you find yourself procrastinating or becoming distracted from what you need to do, take a moment to stop and wash the distractions from your mind by washing your hands with this protective soap.

1. Begin by grating a bar of castile soap until you have one fully packet cup.

2. Heat 3 cups of water to a slight boil and pour into a mixing bowl.

3. Add the soap and mix until the soap is completely melted.

4. Once cool, add the following essential oils, approximately 50–60 drops total:

- Rosemary
- Basil
- Ylang-ylang
- Peppermint

Using a funnel, pour the mixture into a liquid soap dispenser, close the lid tight, and shake vigorously to mix all of the ingredients together. Use to restore focus.

Full Moon Sage Spell

Sage and salt have long been some of the most powerful magic defenses available. Salt is a boundary that dark forces are not able to cross, and burning sage banishes anything negative from your space.

Outside, under the light of the Full Moon, use a sage wand to smudge the area around you while turning counterclockwise. As the sage smoke forms a circle around you, demand that anything wanting to bring harm to you must be gone. Turn twice more, slowly, repeating your demand. Stop at the point where you started

Ask the Goddess Soteria for protection and blessings as you change course and turn clockwise for one full revolution, sprinkling salt around your feet. Thank the goddess for your safety, peace, and health. This spell should be done every Full Moon to prevent harm from coming to you.

Children's Protective Cloak

For those of us who have, or work with, kids, this protective cloak can be summoned to protect them as they move throughout their busy lives. This cloak of light visualization spell will keep children safe when they are away from the home.

Close your eyes and envision the child or children doing their favorite activity, happy and calm. Manifest a light starting from the ground beneath them and imagine it stretching out and up to slowly envelope them. Once they are completely surrounded, imagine the light getting stronger and stronger until you can no longer see the children. Really feel all of the protection that surrounds them, starting with a warmth in your belly and rising to your chest. When ready, say quietly or aloud:

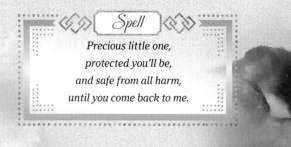

Spell

Precious little one,
protected you'll be,
and safe from all harm,
until you come back to me.

3

Spells to Heal and Prevent Illness

AT SOME POINT IN LIFE, WE'VE ALL encountered something that ails us. You might have physical or spiritual wounds left waiting to heal, you might catch a cold, or maybe you have a seasonal illness. Sickness can take many forms from getting the flu to being heart sick. Let this chapter help ease your hurt and bring you comfort. These spells help heal what ails you, prevent ailments, and help you move forward in a healthier way.

While many of the spells in this chapter focus on various types of healing, from your head to your heart, many of the spells also pertain to preventing a disaster from occurring within you. Oftentimes, we seek help once the damage has been done.

In this chapter you will put your energies into the spells that are preventative. Keeping healthy and staying safe to the best of your ability will always yield the best results as opposed to trying to right a wrong. Broken things can heal, but they come at a cost. They take time, and there's almost always a scar. Think of these spells as a powerful form of self-care.

This chapter is about safeguarding against harm, and a part of remaining safe is about keeping yourself not only physically free from illness, but also taking special care to address your stress and anxiety. In the following pages, you will learn spells to accomplish loving yourself by using breathwork to calm your soul, release limiting beliefs, repair relationships, create curative tonics, and even heal what ails your friends and pets. May you remain healthy, happy, and free from harm.

So mote it be.

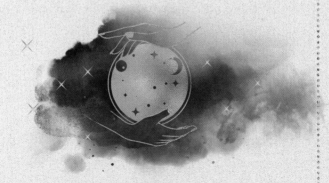

Keeping Everyday Illness and Viruses Away

Sustaining ourselves and our family in good health is important to keeping the home running smoothly and full of good energy vibes. Add a touch of protective energy from the universe to keep illness and viruses away from your home and loved ones. Tuck a clear quartz crystal, the master healer, under your pillow, or turquoise for its overall healing powers. Before that under-the-weather feeling hits, take a moment to actively protect your home.

Spell

I bid you, illness, melt away and leave this house now.
I pray for rest to heal what's left, that life resets its norms.

Easing Aches and Pains

When minor pains distract from your everyday joy or just get in the way of productivity, seek the Moon's healing warmth to ease them. By the Moon's light, set aflame a blue candle. Imagine the Moon's beams gently falling on the area in pain. Feel the warmth radiate through. When ready, say quietly or aloud:

Spell

When aches do slow and pain does grow, I conjure up the sight,
Of warm Moon's glow, and faeries, lo, fair leaping with delight.
O' soothing rays and joyous sight, bring healing with your light.

Breathe Out Stress

A little stress can be an inspiring motivator, but when the pressure builds and threatens to derail you, take a breather to regain your balance.

Choose from these or others you prefer:

♦ Black tea
♦ Chamomile
♦ Ginger, to sip
♦ Lavender, to bathe
♦ Rosemary

Close your eyes and inhale the herbs' rejuvenating scents. Breathe out the stress of the moment. Repeat several times, taking deep mindful breaths. When ready, say quietly:

Spell

Your calming scents do ease my stress and soothe my cares away.
Your leaves relieve my thoughts that tease and tempt my sanity.
Your stems stand strong, to urge me on, to stand and face the fray.

Soul Calming Spell

In addition to performing a soothing ritual, such as Moon Bathing, or working with your calming crystals, this basic spell can help ease your nerves and quiet your soul when there's not time for more. While aligning with the Waning Moon can help your release, use this any time you need to refocus and stay calm.

Take a moment to sit quietly and be still. Close your eyes to shut out any distractions. Focus simply on your natural breathing, being present in the peaceful moment you've created. When ready, say quietly or aloud:

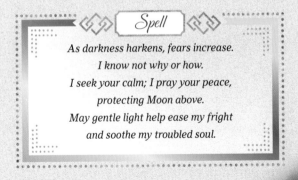

Spell

As darkness harkens, fears increase.
I know not why or how.
I seek your calm; I pray your peace,
protecting Moon above.
May gentle light help ease my fright
and soothe my troubled soul.

Deep Release Cleansing Ritual

There are times when we are holding on to pain and hurt inflicted on us. Other times we might be harboring some limiting beliefs. And other times still, we are besieged by guilt and the need to forgive ourselves. Holding all of these things inside can often manifest as physical illness. This bath ritual can be done to help you deeply reflect on what's vexing you, release the negativity, and to help repair emotional damage.

Use your intuition to decide how much or how little of each ingredient you add.

In a warm bath, intentionally add:

- ◆ Epsom salts
- ◆ Mint
- ◆ Lemon essential oil
- ◆ Ground pepper
- ◆ Dried jasmine flowers
- ◆ White or blue lotus essential oil
- ◆ Calendula
- ◆ Clear quartz
- ◆ Amethyst

Before climbing into the bath to soak, swirl the mixture counterclockwise 7 times with your right hand to raise releasing energy, and say quietly or aloud:

Spell

I release that which is not mine back into the universe.
I release all that is contained in me
that no longer serves me on my divine path.
I acknowledge my pain
and the pain I have caused others
and allow it to dissolve in this water
to make space for healing and growth.
I forgive myself for feeling these things.
I love myself for addressing these things.
I am powerful, and I am cleansed.
So mote it be!

Healing Dream Spell

The versatile amethyst crystal can make people more sensitive to the spiritual realm and also bring about healing. This spell can help with healing a friend, loved one or even yourself. Before bed, draw a warm, soothing bath and add three drops of rose essential oil to the water. Rose oil increases love and happiness, and it opens your heart so you can send them clear, pure healing energy.

Set two amethyst stones in the water and bathe as usual. After you're done, place one of the stones at the foot of your bed and the other under your pillow. Sit on the edge of the bed and think of the person you want healed. Imagine them as perfect, healthy, and whole, doing something they love. Hold the image as long as you can in your mind's eye, and go to bed, contented that they are healed. Their spirit will come to you in a dream, acknowledging that healing has begun.

Self-Love Spray

This is an anytime, anywhere spray used for calming anxieties, keeping negative thoughts at bay, reducing their impact on self-confidence, and bringing more acceptance and self-worth into your daily life.

Begin by lighting a pink candle anointed with coconut oil. In a spray bottle filled halfway with Moon water, add the following oils to your preferred strength: rose for loving energy, neroli to ease anxiety, mimosa for endless self-love, and ylang-ylang to invite the divine feminine energy. Then add:

♦ Crystal Chips
  • Clear Quartz to amplify the spell's energy
  • Rose Quartz for self-love and loving protection
  • Amethyst to relieve stress and anxiety

Hold the bottle in your hands and fill it with accepting, powerful, courageous, uninhibited self-loving energy, then set it next to your candle until it burns out completely.

Relationship Repair Jar

When you want to heal a friendship or romantic relationship, call upon the purifying qualities of salt, the balance of star anise, the energetic healing of peppermint, the love-boosting power of rose petals, and sunflower seeds, which represent joy and better times in the sun. Fill a cleansed jar halfway with salt and intentionally add star anise, peppermint, and rose petals (red for romance, yellow for friendship).

1. Tape two sunflower seeds together. While holding the seeds in your palm, whisper over them:

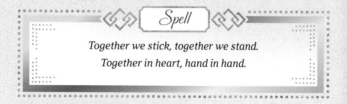

Spell

Together we stick, together we stand.
Together in heart, hand in hand.

2. Place them in the jar and secure the lid, then shake the jar gently, repeating the incantation.

Keep the jar near your altar or workspace, and shake it whenever you think of the other person. The relationship will soon be mended.

Everyday Good Health

Keeping yourself hale and hearty is a matter of practice. This daily spell builds on your own healthy habits with an extra boost of energy. You can do this spell with anything you wear daily. It's more powerful with a pentacle or similar pendant, but you can do it with a watch or other jewelry. If you don't wear jewelry, you can do this spell on your skin by anointing the spot over your heart chakra. Pour a drop of holy or blessed water on your finger. Anoint the pendant with the water while saying quietly or aloud:

Spell

I am healthy.
I am healed.
My best self is revealed.

Healing Fire Tea

Use this tried-and-true kitchen witch healing tea whenever you start feeling cold or flu-like symptoms to nip it in the bud! It's especially great if you have a sore throat or have a persistent cough. This spell contains apple cider vinegar, which is an amazing "cure-all" remedy that kills bacteria, helps balance your internal pH levels, and tastes better than it smells!

Add the following into a mug:

♦ 1 fresh lemon wedge, squeezed and left in the mug
♦ 2 slices of fresh ginger
♦ Local honey or Manuka to taste
♦ 1 tbsp apple cider vinegar

Fill the rest of the mug with hot water (boiled Full Moon water can bring a fantastic healing element) and stir counterclockwise with the intention to allow this mixture to fill you up and rid you of what is ailing you. Kitchen witches recommend drinking 2 cups per day for 3 days for maximum effect, while increasing your water intake to avoid dehydration.

Four Thieves Oil

The history of Four Thieves Oil dates back to the 14th century and the bubonic plague. It is said that four thieves successfully robbed and looted the dead and dying plague victims without catching it themselves. They accomplished this by creating special masks, fashioned to look like the beak-shaped masks doctors wore at that time, imbibed with specific herbs, spices, and oils. The medicinal benefits of the ingredients were proven to kill airborne bacteria and toxic molds, as well as support and bolster the immune system.

In a cleansed glass bottle, intentionally add the following essential oils:

- 15 drops rosemary
- 20 drops clove
- 10 drops cinnamon
- 15 drops eucalyptus
- 10 drops lemon

Fill the bottle with your preferred carrier oil. It can keep for up to a year with proper storage, but always do a sniff test before using to make sure the oil hasn't gone rancid.

Healing Spell for Your Cat

Cats have long been associated with magic, and the Goddess Bast will often look after her tiny charges with compassion and ferocity. This spell is fitting whether you have built a long-term relationship with this goddess, or if you're coming to her for the first time, and naturally it should be used in conjunction with care from your veterinarian.

On your altar, set a small representation of the Goddess Bast in front of a mirror; it can be a small figurine or just a picture. In front of her, place two small offering bowls, one filled with water, the other containing catnip. Sit by the altar and simply tell her about your cat: the cat's name, what he or she looks like, their personality traits, and how they need her help. Tell her how your cat acts when they are healthy, and picture it in your mind. Thank Bast and leave up the altar until your cat is better and has discovered the catnip.

Healing Spell for Your Dog

When our dog is ill, it weighs heavily on our heart and mind. While any healing spell for your pet should be cast in conjunction with good veterinary care, this spell is designed to bring relief to your dog's ailments and a positive diagnosis from the vet. White is a strong color for healing, but it also represents purity, good outcomes, and peace within our hearts.

1. Rub six white birthday candles with coconut oil, which represents protection and is also symbolic as a pet-friendly oil since it is non-toxic for dogs.

2. After the oil has been applied to the candles, hold them in your hand for a moment, with healing thoughts in your heart.

3. Set them in a circle on a plate, and place one of your dog's treats in the middle of the circle.

4. Light the candles, and envision your pup being healthy and happy, and doing what they love best.

5. When the candles are burned out, thank the universe for helping your pup, and offer them a little nibble of the treat.

Sore Throat Tonic

This tonic is stored in the fridge and can be added to tea or taken by the spoonful when needed to rid a sore throat and ease coughing.

Gather:

- 2 peeled and smashed cloves of garlic
- 5 large slices of fresh ginger
- 1" sprig fresh rosemary
- 2" cinnamon stick
- 1 tsp red pepper flakes
- Juice of 1 whole lemon
- 3 tbsp apple cider vinegar
- Honey

Add all the ingredients in a medium-sized jar, and fill the jar with honey until all of the elements are all completely submerged. Stir the mixture in the jar counterclockwise with a tool of your choice, filling it with your intent that this tonic will remove what ails you from your system. Keep it tightly closed and let it sit for 2 days before sipping.

Healing Inside Out

This spell should not be used as a substitute for therapy or mental health care, but it can speed up the process of becoming balanced and restore positive thinking. It can be performed as often as the need arises and relies on the negativity-sucking power of black tourmaline to ground you in day-to-day life.

Light one blue candle and a white candle beside it. In front of the candles, place a pocket-sized black tourmaline stone. Gaze at the candle flames, and see yourself in the best possible light. Feel yourself surrounded by a soft blue and white haze, as it gently washes through you, taking away your sadness, fear or anger. Let the light roll over you, until you begin to feel relief. Extinguish the candles and pick up the black tourmaline. It is now charged, and you can summon the light whenever you need it throughout your day.

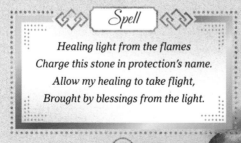

Spell

Healing light from the flames
Charge this stone in protection's name.
Allow my healing to take flight,
Brought by blessings from the light.

Stay Healthy Spell

The humble buckeye nut grows throughout the Midwest and South, and has long had a reputation for boosting health and prosperity. The buckeye, along with black tourmaline, provides a one-two punch for stress and illness in this spell.

1. Start with a small, black box with a lid; it can be wood, cardboard, whatever you have handy.

2. Pour salt in the box until the bottom is covered, then place a black tourmaline stone in it.

3. At least once a week, open the box gently, lower your face to it and speak all your complaints, worries, and problems inside it.

4. After you're done, close the box quickly.

The salt, stone, and color of the box will absorb your troubles, while carrying a buckeye through the day will bring health and better fortune. Once a month, change out the salt in the box and recharge the black tourmaline for one week in the sunshine.

Black Walnut Spell

Here we use black walnut and the number 5—symbolizing freedom, curiosity, and change—to brush away the internal cobwebs and make more room for illuminating light to come in.

Take five walnuts and gently brush the dirt and any remaining hull from them. For five nights, under a Waning Moon, go outside and stand in the moonlight. Take one walnut and pass it lightly over the afflicted area if you need healing, or over the body in general to absorb any discomfort that may be building while saying quietly or aloud:

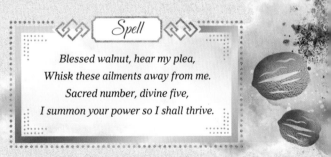

Spell

Blessed walnut, hear my plea,
Whisk these ailments away from me.
Sacred number, divine five,
I summon your power so I shall thrive.

At the end of five nights, bury the five walnuts out in nature and walk away without looking back. Your pain or illness will soon ease.

Love Thyself Oil

This oil can be used to anoint candles in self-love and healing rituals, to anoint charms to help bring more self-love into your life, to diffuse into the air via heat or water, and can be worn directly on the skin.

In a bottle, add 1 dried rosebud and 7 drops each of:

♦ Mimosa flower to lift your mood
♦ Ylang-ylang for peace
♦ Rose to look at yourself through the eyes of love
♦ Neroli for courage, and good fortune

Fill the bottle nearly to the top with your preferred carrier oil. While holding the bottle close to your heart to charge and activate the oil, say quietly or aloud:

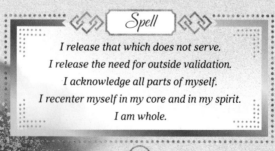

Spell

I release that which does not serve.
I release the need for outside validation.
I acknowledge all parts of myself.
I recenter myself in my core and in my spirit.
I am whole.

Bringing Family
Back Together

Trees are graceful, strong, and their roots reach deeply into the earth. They may sway with the winds, but they survive year after year to bless us with their beauty and magic. Your family tree, while metaphorical, can be just as connected and strong as the trees outside your window.

To heal strife in your family or bring the family back together, gather:

♦ Handful of acorns
♦ Black marker
♦ Small piece of bark from a tree in your yard

Write each family member's name on an acorn with the marker, then draw a heart on the interior of the bark. It doesn't have to be perfect or legible, the important part is that you know it's there. Bury the acorns and the bark together in the back yard. Your family will begin to draw closer together, forgiving old wounds and making fresh, wonderful new memories.

Feet on the Earth Grounding Oil

Chances are, if you are feeling frazzled or stressed, having difficulty focusing, or feel like you're making a lot of mistakes you typically wouldn't make, you could probably use some grounding. Sometimes we get so caught up in our minds, thinking about the past and the future, that we forget about the present "right now" and essentially disconnect our minds from our bodies. That tends to cause physical manifestations of generally feeling not so great and perhaps you're not sure why.

Grounding can be easily achieved by putting your bare feet on the earth, or by touching something in nature with your hands and sitting deep within that moment. This oil recipe helps realign a possibly blocked root chakra and helps reconnect your mind and body to renew a sense of stability and centering within yourself. The smell of this oil is extremely important, since it's recommended that you wear it as a perfume and dabbed on the front and back of your root chakra. It should bring a sense of calm and awareness. Feel free to adjust ingredient quantities to achieve that sensation.

Gather:

- Herbs
- Hibiscus
- Rosemary
- Yarrow
- Lavender
- Chamomile
- Jasmine
- Rose petals
- 1–2 small shell pieces
- 1 small piece of tourmalinated quartz

Essential Oils

- 13 drops rose
- 15 drops jasmine
- 15 drops lavender
- 2 drops frankincense

Add all of the elements to a cleansed jar. Fill with preferred carrier oil almost to the top, close the lid, and shake gently to combine. This is when you smell the oil and adjust as necessary to achieve a grounding sensation. Write your magical recipe in your spell journal so you can recreate it when you run low.

Energy Storage

Filling quartz with your best intentions, energies, and feelings gives you something to draw from if you're feeling a little under the weather.

Choose a large quartz crystal and place it in the sunshine for seven days to cleanse. After that, place it in the light of a Waxing Moon for seven nights to charge. Using a cotton ball, lightly rub it with a diluted mix of peppermint and clove essential oils. When you are having a lovely day, relax, hold the crystal and say quietly:

Spell

I always have my health.
Good health is easy to find.
It's always right here,
ready to ease my mind.

On days when you feel low, take the crystal out and feel the energy surging into you.

Aloe Vera
Healing Protection

Aloe heals, enhances beauty, offers protection, and brings luck. Grown on a windowsill, aloe guards the home against evil and accidents and attracts luck. Use the gel of the leaves to soothe burns and bug bites and help heal just about any minor cut or scratch. Rub a bit of the plant's gel on a white candle and burn it safely for a healing spell. Then speak this incantation aloud:

Spell

Candle white, burn so bright, reveal your healing message now.
Aloe gel, join this spell, reach deep within your curing well
of healing balm and soothing calm that everything will soon be well.

Soothing Grief

While grief is a process that can take years, or even a lifetime, call on this spell when you're feeling overwhelmed with loss and sadness in the moment.

On your altar, lay out several items that represent happy or loving memories with what or whom you're grieving. Anoint a pale blue candle with your favorite essential oil and light it while you reflect on the beautiful memories. Don't hold back on expressing your emotions; cry, laugh, sing, or just breathe deeply. When ready, say quietly or aloud:

Spell

This is the hardest thing I've done—my grief does overwhelm.
For loss has changed my life in ways before not ever known.
I sit, fair Moon, before your grace and wonder at your sight,
    will beauty touch my life again—beyond this fleeting sight?
The Moon, she answers, "Yes, it will." And time, it helps to heal.
Return each night. We'll gaze—delight—at what this peace reveals.

All Moon Healing Ritual

The Full Moon is optimal for healing and protection from illness, but the New Moon and Waxing Moon phases should not be overlooked. Feeling the full weight of the Moon's energy, breathe deeply to fill your body from head to toe with her warmth. Reflect on what needs to be healed and create a picture in your mind of what that looks like. Keeping the picture in focus, when ready, say quietly or aloud:

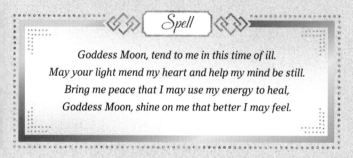

Spell

Goddess Moon, tend to me in this time of ill.
May your light mend my heart and help my mind be still.
Bring me peace that I may use my energy to heal,
Goddess Moon, shine on me that better I may feel.

When finished, remain quiet and remind yourself of the picture you had in your head. Take a moment to honor your courage and thank the Moon for her light.

Inner Goddess Strength

Summon your inner goddess strength and sit with any goddess of healing that resonates with you. Airmid is a favorite for her vast herbal healing knowledge and compassion.

Gather a black candle for protection or a green candle to channel the herbs Airmid works with, an amethyst or clear quartz crystal for its healing energies, and any healing herbs you can, such as angelica, bay leaf, fennel, ivy, lemon balm, or marigold. Essential oils can stand in—try chamomile, lavender, rose, sandalwood, or peppermint.

1. Anoint the candle with essential oil. Light the candle.

2. Muddle or crush the fresh herbs in your cauldron, if you have one, to release their healing oils, aromas, and energies.

3. Take a deep breath in and hold it, letting the herbal energies and the life-sustaining oxygen reach deep throughout your body. Exhale slowly.

Continue to breathe this way, focusing your breath and its healing energies on the part of your body that you wish to heal, including your mind, heart, or soul. When ready, say quietly or aloud:

Spell

That which heals can also harm,
respect I must these herbal balms.
With thoughts attuned to easing pain,
I pray your healing hands to lay
upon my [area to be healed],
draw ills away and speed release, to mend I may.
The body may be first to feel but mind
and heart are next to heal.
With time, as wounds do fade away,
I'll not forget your help this day.

Summon Healing Spirits

When you or someone you love is ailing, turn to the powerful spirits of healing for this ritual. The best outcomes for rituals like this happen when working on your own behalf, but when only healing is intended, you may also perform this on behalf of others.

> On your altar, gather:
>
> ◆ Almonds, as an offering to invoke the healing powers of the spirits
> ◆ Small glass of pure water
> ◆ 1 blue (calming energy) or red (warming energy) candle for healing

1. Place the almonds and water on your altar as an offering.

2. Light the candle; its energy will help release your prayer into the world. Take a moment in silent meditation to call forth the spirits whose healing powers you seek. Visualize them with you. Acknowledge their presence.

3. On your paper, write down the specific illness and symptoms that you wish to be relieved, as well as what you desire to replace them. Fold the paper as small as you can and place it into the cauldron on a heatproof surface and burn it.

Pray to the spirits for healing relief by saying quietly or aloud:

Spell

O' Mighty Spirits I feel your healing light.
Place your curing
touch upon [name] to dispel the ills that grip.
With water from your sacred font,
do purify the wounds you see and those that hide inside.
Bring peaceful thoughts to ease
the fear and help to calm the dread.
With breath of life do sing of times
when health and joy resume.
Please banish pain and restore
strength that healing does ensue.
For this we honor you, give thanks, for what we ask of you.

4

Spells
for Good
Luck

ONE OF THE BEST WAYS TO STOP negative energies from creeping into your life is with luck spells. If your days are filled with good luck, there's simply no room for harm to take up residence. The purpose of the spells in this chapter is two-fold: First, to summon good luck. Then, there's protection from bad luck.

Begin with taking assessment of your last week, month, or year. What has gone wrong? What has gone right? What do you need to happen next? Be sure to journal these things out, as written records of what you've done and need to do are essential to spellwork.

Once that is done, sit with yourself and try to assess not only your energy, but the energy that surrounds you. Some of us attract energy vampires who suck the life out of us, and some of us attract negative energies. Knowing what can and has blocked you in the past can help open the doors not only for a brighter future, but for successful luck spells.

In this chapter, there are a variety of spells that cover all kinds of luck, from monetary to well wishes. Additionally, there are lucky oil recipes and chants to help crowd out negativity. Thank the goddess or the universe for the good things that have come your way thus far before you begin, and after your spells have been completed. There are so many things to be thankful for. More than anything else, gratitude makes room for more good things to enter your life.

Be well.

So mote it be.

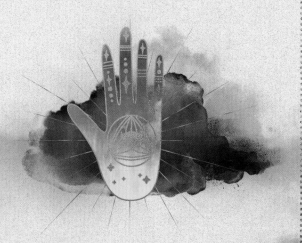

Clear Negative Energy

Sometimes, what seems like a run of bad luck or misfortune is really just the need to become unstuck. Cleansing our psyches can clear the effects of accumulated negative energies that may be holding us back. Evoke any Moon goddess who can join you at the height of the Full Moon, when her purifying energy is at its highest, to cleanse, restore, and celebrate the ritual of making room for new, positive energies to fill you.

Call on your goddess and sit with her in meditation. Breathe deeply in. Slowly out. Again. Focus your thoughts on filling your body with the goddess's flowing vitality on every breath in. Let yourself feel it travel throughout your body. Breathe out any negativity. When ready, say to your goddess quietly or aloud:

Spell

As air flows in and feeds my lungs
your love flows in to feed the soul.
Each breath replaces dark with light that flows
through me with cleansing might—
the rhythm of my life's restored,
with humble thanks, you are adored.

Wealthy Comfrey

Comfrey symbolizes hearth and home—its message is one of welcome. Comfrey offers protection for travelers and their luggage. It helps with healing and brings love and money—especially lucky gambling—into your life.

Carry a piece of comfrey root in your wallet to encourage wealth. Grow the plant near your home's entrances to ward off evil and ghosts who lurk. Add it to a spell jar or bag to draw in what you desire. Add the blossoms to a ritual bath when your focus is setting boundaries and protecting your privacy. When your concentration is set, your visualization for boundaries strong, say the following chant quietly or aloud:

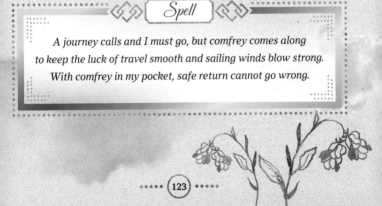

Spell

A journey calls and I must go, but comfrey comes along
to keep the luck of travel smooth and sailing winds blow strong.
With comfrey in my pocket, safe return cannot go wrong.

Round Robin Wishes

Open a window and let the robin's uplifting voice sing to life's celebrations! This is a powerful time to make a wish—over a lost tooth, birthday candles, a shooting star, or for something bigger like finding a new home or true love. No matter the object of your lucky desires, let Mrs. Robin lend a hand. Over the melodious chirping of birds, speak the following chant:

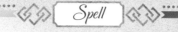

Spell

Chirp, trill, burble, tweet—
What cheerful song you sing.
For though not Irish of descent,
The luck you bring is sweet.
So, chirp, trill, burble, tweet from sunrise to sunset . . .
Each lovely note a penny dropped into my wishing well.

Abundance of Success

Basil is a favorite of kitchen witches for its abundant magical properties: business, fortune, luck, love, prosperity, and courage. This is a powerful yet simple spell involving basil and shared abundance, but it requires specific conditions. For this spell, the basil must be given to you by a friend; it can be loose leaves or a live plant, but it must come from someone else's generosity.

First, thank your friend for their thoughtfulness. Place the basil near where you spend most of your time. After it is in place, thank the spirit of the plant for coming to you and bringing you new opportunities and good luck, then speak the incantation below. Both you and your friend will quickly see money and career success flowing into your lives.

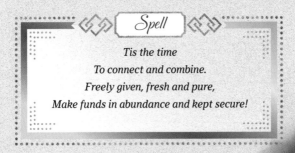

Spell

Tis the time
To connect and combine.
Freely given, fresh and pure,
Make funds in abundance and kept secure!

Turn Around Your Fortunes

Use this spell when you feel that you've been facing too many unforeseen challenges. For best outcomes, bring openness and creativity to this ritual, allowing yourself to be led by an optimistic action of change, rather than through resentment or pessimism.

Gather:

♦ One or more pieces of litter,
   such as discarded paper
♦ A visual of your desired outcome
♦ Pen and paper
♦ A candle

1. On your paper, write down your desired outcome. For best outcomes, this should apply solely to the person performing the ritual and not wish ill on anyone else. Light the candle.

2. Light the paper in your cauldron and watch the flames turn your intentions into fertile ash.

Envision yourself capable of creating change and calling on your own powers to shift your reality to the best possible version of itself. When ready, say quietly or aloud:

Spell

*From the ground I thee pluck
this little bit of turnaround luck.
Forgotten and discarded
into something still regarded,
this trash into treasure
in my fortune I will find pleasure.*

Extinguish the candle and watch the rising smoke take your prayer into the cosmos, where it will be received and answered.

Crown of Success Oil

An extremely energetic good luck oil, Crown of Success brings overall good fortune in life, and helps encourage victory in your endeavors. This is best made during the Waxing Moon.

Gather:

♦ Myrrh resin – to attract your desires
♦ Bay leaf – for protection and victory
♦ Star Anise – commands leadership and confidence
♦ Whole cloves – to open the way to sweet things
♦ Dried orange peel – to encourage success
♦ 13 drops sandalwood oil for abundance
♦ 1 small seashell for the pulling away of obstacles
♦ 1 small piece of amber – for attracting energy

Add each ingredient to the bottle, then fill with carrier oil. Hold the jar to your solar plexus and say quietly or aloud:

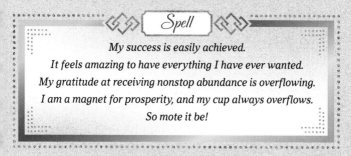

Spell

My success is easily achieved.
It feels amazing to have everything I have ever wanted.
My gratitude at receiving nonstop abundance is overflowing.
I am a magnet for prosperity, and my cup always overflows.
So mote it be!

Leave this oil out in sunlight for 3 days. Then put in a dark place and let sit for at least 3 weeks, shaking every 5 or so days before use.

Quick Luck
Basil Bloom Bag

Basil is extremely easy to grow, whether you plant it in an outdoor garden, or in a pot indoors. Occasionally your basil plants will sprout small, white blooms, perfect for representing new growth in your life.

Pinch them off the plant and drop in a small mesh bag, or fold some cheesecloth over them and secure at the top with a string. Inhale the rich aroma and recite this incantation:

Spell

Bloom in spirit, your power is strong.
Bring me the best luck all day long.
Basil with your herbal song,
Bring your luck to help me along.

Clover Fairy Spell

Bay leaf can purify a space, bring a wish to fulfillment, and draw prosperity to you, usually through the speed of fire magic. It's especially effective when you need something in a pinch or some quick luck for the household. Clover boosts success and is a powerful plant of the fairy world. Using bay leaves and clover together intertwines the magic of wishes and builds a positive working relationship with the fae. Gather:

- ♦ Four bay leaves
- ♦ Handful of clover
- ♦ Lighter or matches
- ♦ Heat safe container

1. Write your intention on each of the bay leaves.

2. Once dusk has fallen, burn one bay leaf every 15 minutes until the four leaves are gone.

3. Wait until the residue has completely cooled, then mix it with a handful of fresh clover and set it outside in a small offering dish near the back door.

The nearby fae will see your need and begin their work to expedite the bay leaves' magic for you. Once you receive it, leave a small offering of milk to thank them for their help.

Mighty Good Luck Oil

This oil is excellent for use in any prosperity, success, protection, or luck spellwork. It can also be used to anoint money to encourage wealth to flow to you, or wear as a perfume when you need a bit of extra luck. This is best made at night, during the New Moon. This oil will take some time to make, and the spell relies on your intuition, so no measured amounts are included. Use as much or as little as you feel called to.

Gather:

- Herbs
- Cinnamon
- Lavender
- Cloves
- Chamomile
- Sunflower petals
- Dried orange peels
- Essential oils
- Ginger
- Frankincense
- Lavender
- Sandalwood
- Geranium
- Crystal Chips (optional)
- Tiger's Eye
- Citrine
- Clear Quartz

With your intention in mind, mindfully add each of the ingredients to the bottle and fill it nearly to the top with carrier oil. Place the lid on tightly then hold the bottle to your solar plexus and say quietly or aloud:

Spell

Prosperity and success
flow in like an unending river.
I always feel fulfilled.
I am never left wanting for anything.
Opportunities come into my life
effortlessly and quickly.
I release my expectations for success.
I trust in my divine path and the guidance
of my spirits and ancestors.
Things always come easy to me.
My life is prosperous.
So mote it be!

Once completed, leave the bottle out under the New Moon overnight, and keep it out in the sunlight for another 3 days. Move it to somewhere dark and let sit for 1 full moon cycle before using.

Golden Egg Spell

The secular inspiration for the Easter celebration is found in the pagan holiday Ostara, represented by fertile symbols like blossoming flowers, ever-reproducing bunnies, and the egg, a literal promise of life and hope. During the Easter season, a variety of fillable, reusable eggs are available in stores, including eggs that are bright and gold-colored. You'll need a golden egg for each member of the household, and a pen and paper.

Each person should take a slip of paper and write their full name across it. Flip the paper over and write down the type of good luck they seek. It can be good luck for bringing in money, for success, for health, or whatever they might desire. When they are done, roll the paper up to bring the luck toward you and place it inside each golden egg. If you feel inspired, each person can choose an herb and add a plume or pinch of it to their egg. Collect everyone's golden eggs and store them near a door to call in the luck. Make it a lovely new tradition by reusing the eggs and making new requests each spring!

Fehu Abundance

When you need some extra energy to bring good luck and abundance or a desire you want to manifest, utilize the power of an Elder Furthark rune.

Fehu

Abundance; Hope; Plenty; Success; Happiness

Gather:

♦ Red candle, and a sharp carving tool
♦ Success, prosperity, or road-opening oil of your choice
♦ Mint, cinnamon, basil, and salt, ground together

1. Using your sharp tool carve the rune Fehu on the surface of your candle, chanting the name. Continue until your candle is completely covered with the symbol, anoint with oil and dress with the ground herbs.

2. Place the candle in a fire safe vessel, and surround it with a protective circle of salt. Let it burn out naturally.

Road Opening Oil

This oil's purpose is to bust open any blockages or obstacles that might be hindering you from reaching a goal, receiving abundance from the universe, or blocking new possible avenues for success. It is best made during a New Moon and should be used for ritual work only. Do not diffuse this oil into the air or wear it on your body.

Gather:

- Herbs
- Bay leaves
- Rose petals
- Lavender
- Calendula
- Yarrow
- Mint
- Lemon Verbena
- Damiana
- Hibiscus

Essential Oils

- 7 drops frankincense
- 7 drops peppermint
- 7 drops rose
- 13 drops sandalwood
- 13 drops lavender
- 13 drops honeysuckle

Mindfully add each ingredient to a jar, then fill nearly to the top with carrier oil. Once closed, hold the jar to your solar plexus and say quietly or aloud:

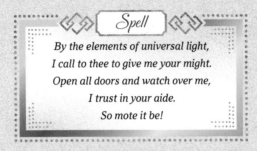

Spell

By the elements of universal light,
I call to thee to give me your might.
Open all doors and watch over me,
I trust in your aide.
So mote it be!

Once completed, store in a dark place for a minimum of 3 weeks before using. Take the jar out and shake it every 5 days.

Sneaky Luck Oil

This oil can be used in any prosperity, success, protection, or luck spellwork, but witches have the most fun using this to secretly bring luck and success to people and spaces around them. Sneakily, place a drop on your finger and dab as you walk past the doorway of your office, dab on the boardroom table before a big meeting, dab as you walk through a doorway to confront a tough situation, or even dab on a friend's belongings to bring them luck. Use as much or as little of the herbs and oils as you feel called to.

Gather:

- Cinnamon
- Lavender
- Clove

Essential oils

- Ginger
- Lavender
- Sandalwood

Crystal Chips

- Tiger's Eye
- Citrine
- Clear Quartz

Mindfully add each ingredient to the bottle with your intention in mind, then fill the bottle with carrier oil. Secure the lid, then hold the bottle to your solar plexus and say quietly or aloud:

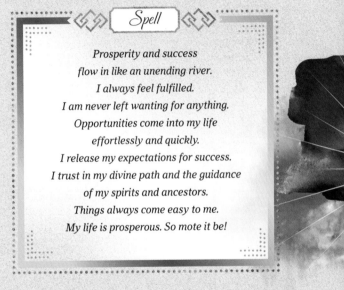

Spell

Prosperity and success
flow in like an unending river.
I always feel fulfilled.
I am never left wanting for anything.
Opportunities come into my life
effortlessly and quickly.
I release my expectations for success.
I trust in my divine path and the guidance
of my spirits and ancestors.
Things always come easy to me.
My life is prosperous. So mote it be!

Once completed, leave the bottle out under the New Moon overnight, and keep it out in the sunlight for another 3 days. Move it to somewhere dark and let sit for 1 full moon cycle before using.

Casino Luck Oil

Citrus-scented essential oils such as orange, grapefruit and lemongrass are associated with luck, positive emotions and prosperity, which makes them an excellent base for a powerful good luck oil. Add in chicory, which has a reputation for removing obstacles, plus the dandelion's qualities of healing and granting wishes. Use this oil in casting luck spells, or take some with you to the casino for an added boost of money luck.

Gather:

- Orange essential oil
- Grapefruit essential oil
- Lemongrass essential oil
- A thin strip of dried chicory root
- Dried dandelion petals
- A 4 oz. bottle with cap or stopper
- Small oil dropper

1. Insert the dried ingredients into the bottle first, thanking them for bringing you good luck at the casino or wherever you need it.

2. Add three drops each of orange, grapefruit and lemongrass essential oils.

3. Fill nearly to the top with the carrier oil of your choice, leaving some room so you can easily shake the bottle and mix the ingredients. Secure the cap, and hold the bottle in both hands while expressing gratitude for all the positive energy coming your way.

Divine Orange Protection

A divine fruit, oranges have delighted people long before they were as widely available as they are today. Once reserved as a special Christmas time treat in Europe, they helped to prevent scurvy in the long winter months. While we may not need them to ward off scurvy these days, they can still help us in warding off bad luck.

To clear your space of bad energy and call in good luck, boil two sliced oranges, one sliced lemon, two cinnamon sticks, a smattering of cloves, cranberries, and enough water to cover it all. As you stir your infusion clockwise, say quietly or aloud:

Spell

With ample offering of fruit and spice
I bless this space free from vice
Welcome are those who come to share
both mirth and glee, sorrow and scare
for with the support of each other
there is no storm for us to weather

Lucky Lavender

While this veritable herb is typically known for its calming scent and protective energies, it is also a powerful ingredient to add to your prosperity, luck, and success arsenal.

Here are some uses for lavender in the realm of luck:

- Sprinkle a few dried buds in your wallet to draw money
- Add the dried buds to any prosperity workings you do
- Diffuse lavender oil into the air via heat or a water diffuser
- Burn cut and fully dried stalks with the bud still attached in for manifestation
- Add dried lavender to your sage wand and burn to cleanse

Sweeten Your Life

Just as you can't be impatient while adding honey to any recipe, you can't be impatient with this honey jar. Trust that it will take the time it needs to do what it needs to do. The results are always worth the wait. You will need a pink candle for love, and a white candle for healing. Gather:

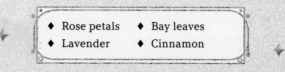

- Rose petals
- Lavender
- Bay leaves
- Cinnamon

Add each ingredient mindfully to your jar, then fill with honey until all ingredients are covered. Affix your candles to the top of the lid, light them, and allow them to burn down completely. As you light the candles, say quietly:

Spell

Kindness grows inside our heart
All our differences fall apart.
Sweetness shining like the sun,
Send good to all, and harm no one.
So mote it be!

Revitalize Gratitude

Sometimes we lose sight of the blessings that already abound in our lives. This ritual calls for the abundance available to us to present itself easily and swiftly to remind us that we have much to be grateful for.

Take time to picture all of the blessings you already have; you can think of your home, a best friend who supports you, a job you find rewarding, the food you eat every day, and even the small things, like the companionship of your pet. Feel the warmth of gratitude wash over you, as the universe has given you so much abundance. When you are ready, say three times:

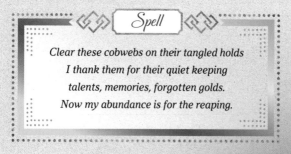

Spell

Clear these cobwebs on their tangled holds
I thank them for their quiet keeping
talents, memories, forgotten golds.
Now my abundance is for the reaping.

7 Days to Ongoing Prosperity

Burn this candle as a repellant from bad luck and failure, or burn in conjunction with other prosperity spellwork for extra energy.

You will need a plain jar candle, preferably green, but white always works. Create your own sigil to put on the glass to fix the intention.

1. Affix your sigil to the front of your cleansed candle. Be creative, and don't be afraid to be simple or extravagantly artistic! You can use a sharpie or acrylic paint to draw it on.

2. Take a thin sharp object like a toothpick or unbent paper clip to poke 3 holes ½ inch deep into the top of the candle.

3. Place the candle in the center of a plate, and surround it with bay leaves, orange peels, basil, cinnamon, and crushed egg shells.

4. Add 13 drops of prosperity oil to the top of the candle, using your finger to swirl clockwise pushing the oil into the holes, and to bring in attracting energy.

Spell

As this candle burns, prosperity comes in effortlessly.

An air of success is present in my life at all times.

I always feel fulfilled.

Opportunities come into my life effortlessly and quickly.

Aphrodite in Love

Beyond being a tasty addition to different dishes, rosemary is a symbol of fidelity and true love. It is said to be a sign of a lasting relationship when a piece from a bride's bouquet is planted and successfully grows. In some cultures, people have slept with rosemary tucked under their pillows, hoping that the plant will reveal the identity of their soulmate in their dreams.

If you're looking to call in luck in love, whether new or old, turn to Aphrodite, the Goddess of Love, for this ritual.

Gather:

♦ Rosemary
♦ Small glass of pure water
♦ Goddess Aphrodite statue or picture
♦ A candle or incense

1. Place the rosemary and water on your altar next to the image of Aphrodite.

2. Light the candle with the intention of opening a channel of communication with Aphrodite.

3. On your paper, write out the qualities you need to feel loved.

Allow the words of your prayer to mix with the gentle rise of your candle's smoke, and when ready say:

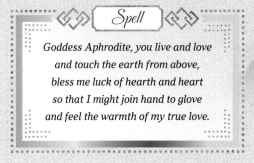

Spell

*Goddess Aphrodite, you live and love
and touch the earth from above,
bless me luck of hearth and heart
so that I might join hand to glove
and feel the warmth of my true love.*

4. Fold the paper as small as you can, infusing each fold with good intentions.

5. Offer the paper to the flame and open yourself up to receive the love you ask for.

Malachite Jar

Sand is used for money work, since the coins we wish for are as countless as its grains. Glitter has a magical component we rarely think about—it sticks around forever, popping up when you least expect it!

Gather

- Cup of sand
- ½ cup of glitter (gold, green, or both)
- Mid-sized malachite stone

1. Write your name on a slip of paper, then reverse it and write "Come to me" on the back.

2. Wrap the paper around the malachite and place it in the bottom of a jar.

3. Pour in the sand until the malachite is covered. Add the glitter on top and mix it slightly with the sand.

Spell

Money comes, money stays,
money brings, money pays.

Favorable Outcome

Have you ever picked up a found lucky penny? Tossed a coin into a wishing well? These are forms of coin magic, a powerful form of mysticism that we use to cast a favorable outcome.

For this spell, you'll need two half-dollar coins, and two white spell candles. Place one coin face up under the first candle, and the second coin face down under the second candle. Make sure the candles are stable with the coins underneath.

Light the candles and speak this incantation:

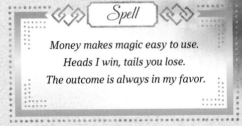

Spell

Money makes magic easy to use.
Heads I win, tails you lose.
The outcome is always in my favor.

Allow the first candle to burn down entirely after blowing out the second candle.

Curse Removal

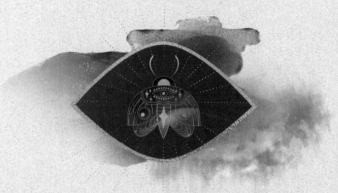

Whether you have a curse put on you by another witch, or just a build up of negativity use this luck spell to dispel bad luck and draw positivity toward you. The mirror will reflect the curse of bad luck away from you and prevent it from coming back.

On your altar, gather a lit green candle, salt, cinnamon, and a mirror. Imagine that there is a circle of light on the floor around you. Visualize every instance of recent bad luck as if it were a small dark bundle on the floor surrounding you. Pick each one up and mindfully place it outside the circle of light. Once all of the bundles are outside your circle, imagine that they turn to smoke and dissolve in to the air.

1. Place the mirror behind the candle, facing away from you.

2. Spread salt in a circle around the candle and chant:

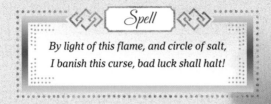

> ### Spell
>
> *By light of this flame, and circle of salt,*
> *I banish this curse, bad luck shall halt!*

3. Sprinkle the cinnamon around the salt. Say:

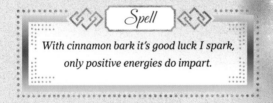

> ### Spell
>
> *With cinnamon bark it's good luck I spark,*
> *only positive energies do impart.*

Allow the candle to burn all the way down. You should see a turn around in your luck almost immediately.

Conclusion

As your journey with this book of protection spells concludes, keep in mind that they can be revisited any time you need protection or luck. Spellwork relies on the power of your intuition, so if ever you feel that a spell needs to be adjusted or personalized, that's exactly what you must do. Continue to learn about and connect with your Goddesses, as they are your guides. Remember to honor your ancestors, for they are your wisdom. And continue to trust in yourself, for your Higher Self is your truth.

In closing, here are some tips to keep in mind as you practice and grow your own personal brand of magic:

Always practice self-assessment. There is no such thing as too much self-assessment. Evaluations help to ground us and let us know where to place our next steps. Evaluate where you are, how you feel, and what you need.

Do your journaling. Be it related to spellcasting or for your own peace of mind, journaling helps bring clarity. Clarity is of the utmost importance of spellcasting; I cannot reiterate this enough! If our intents are murky, then so are our spells, which leads to not-so-fun results (to say the least). Be clear with yourself; write things out. This will also help with your assessment process.

And finally, always prioritize self-care. This can take many forms: meditation, a fun activity that gets your body moving, stretching, eating well, and being kind to yourself. All these things lead to a happier and healthier you.

So mote it be.

Spell Index

The Quarto Group

Inspiring | Educating | Creating | Entertaining

Brimming with creative inspiration, how-to projects, and useful information to enrich your everyday life, quarto.com is a favorite destination for those pursuing their interests and passions.

First published in 2022, by Wellfleet, an imprint of The Quarto Group, 142 West 36th Street, 4th Floor, New York, NY 10018, USA
T (212) 779-4972 F (212) 779-6058 www.Quarto.com

Contains content previously published in 2020 as *Moon Magic* and *House Magic*, in 2021 as *Herbal Magic*, and in 2022 as *Goddess Magic* by Wellfleet Press, an imprint of The Quarto Group, 142 West 36th Street, 4th Floor, New York, NY 10018, USA.

Wellfleet titles are also available at discount for retail, wholesale, promotional, and bulk purchase. For details, contact the Special Sales Manager by email at specialsales@quarto.com or by mail at The Quarto Group, Attn: Special Sales Manager, 100 Cummings Center Suite 265D, Beverly, MA 01915, USA.

10 9 8 7 6 5 4 3 2 1

ISBN: 978-1-57715-312-2

Library of Congress Cataloging-in-Publication Data

Names: Kane, Aurora, author.
Title: Protection spells : an enchanting spell book to clear negative
  energy / Aurora Kane.
Description: New York, NY, USA : Wellfleet Press, [2022] | Series: Pocket
  spell books | Includes index. | Summary: "Protection Spells is a
  pocket-size volume of charms, rituals, and spells to protect you from
  heartbreak, physical danger, and illness"-- Provided by publisher.
Identifiers: LCCN 2022001400 (print) | LCCN 2022001401 (ebook) | ISBN
  9781577153122 (hardcover) | ISBN 9780760376362 (ebook)
Subjects: LCSH: Incantations. | Charms. | Medicine, Magic, mystic, and
  spagiric. | Rituals. | Self-care, Health--Miscellanea.
Classification: LCC BF1558 .K34 2022 (print) | LCC BF1558 (ebook) | DDC
  133.4/4--dc23/eng/20220225
LC record available at https://lccn.loc.gov/2022001400
LC ebook record available at https://lccn.loc.gov/2022001401

Publisher: Rage Kindelsperger
Creative Director: Laura Drew
Managing Editor: Cara Donaldson
Project Editor: Sara Bonacum
Cover and Interior Design: Evelin Kasikov

Printed in China

Continue your on-the-go spellcraft with additional companions
in the Pocket Spell Books series:

Love Spells

An Enchanting Spell Book
of Potions & Rituals

978-1-57715-314-6

Moon Spells

An Enchanting Spell Book
of Magic & Rituals

978-1-57715-313-9

And coming soon…

Candle Magic
978-1-57715-336-8

Angel Numbers
978-1-57715-339-9

Pendulum Magic
978-1-57715-338-2